Health and Your Body

First Aid Basics

by Rebecca Weber

Content Consultant:
Beth Lapp
Director of Operations
American Red Cross
South Central Minnesota chapter

Pebble Plus is published by Capstone Press,
1710 Roe Crest Drive, North Mankato, Minnesota 56003.
www.capstonepub.com

Books published by Capstone Press are manufactured with paper
containing at least 10 percent post-consumer waste.

Library of Congress Cataloging-in-Publication Data
Weber, Rebecca.
  First aid basics / by Rebecca Weber.
    p. cm. — (Pebble plus. Health and your body)
  Includes bibliographical references and index.
  Summary: "Color photos and simple text describe first aid for cuts, bee stings, choking, and other medical issues"—
Provided by publisher.
  ISBN 978-1-4296-7695-3 (library binding) — ISBN 978-1-4296-7904-6 (paperback)
  1. First aid in illness and injury—Juvenile literature. 2. Medical emergencies—Juvenile literature. I. Title.
  RC86.5.W417 2012
  616.02'52—dc23   2011029913

Editorial Credits
Gillia Olson, editor; Juliette Peters, designer; Wanda Winch, media researcher; Sarah Schuette, photo stylist;
    Marcy Morin, studio scheduler; Kathy McColley, production specialist

Photo Credits
All images by Capstone Studio: Karon Dubke except: iStockphoto: Rich Legg, cover; Photo Researcher, Inc:
    Scott Camazine, 15

Note to Parents and Teachers

The Health and Your Body series supports national science standards related to health and
physical education. This book describes and illustrates basic first aid. The images support early
readers in understanding the text. The repetition of words and phrases helps early readers learn
new words. This book also introduces early readers to subject-specific vocabulary words, which are
defined in the Glossary section. Early readers may need assistance to read some words and to use
the Table of Contents, Glossary, Read More, Internet Sites, and Index sections of the book.

Printed in the United States of America in North Mankato, Minnesota.
102011
006405CGS12

Table of Contents

First Aid

Have you ever scraped a knee?
You may have gotten first aid.
First aid is help for hurt people
when a doctor or trained
medical person is not there.

Calling for Help

The first step is to get adult help.
When someone is badly hurt,
call 911 for help. Badly hurt
people shouldn't be moved
unless they are in danger.

Don't Touch Blood

People giving first aid shouldn't touch blood with bare hands. Blood can carry diseases. People use gloves or another barrier before touching blood.

Cuts and Scrapes

Cuts and scrapes first need to be washed with soap and water. A clean cloth or bandage pressed firmly on a cut or scrape can stop bleeding.

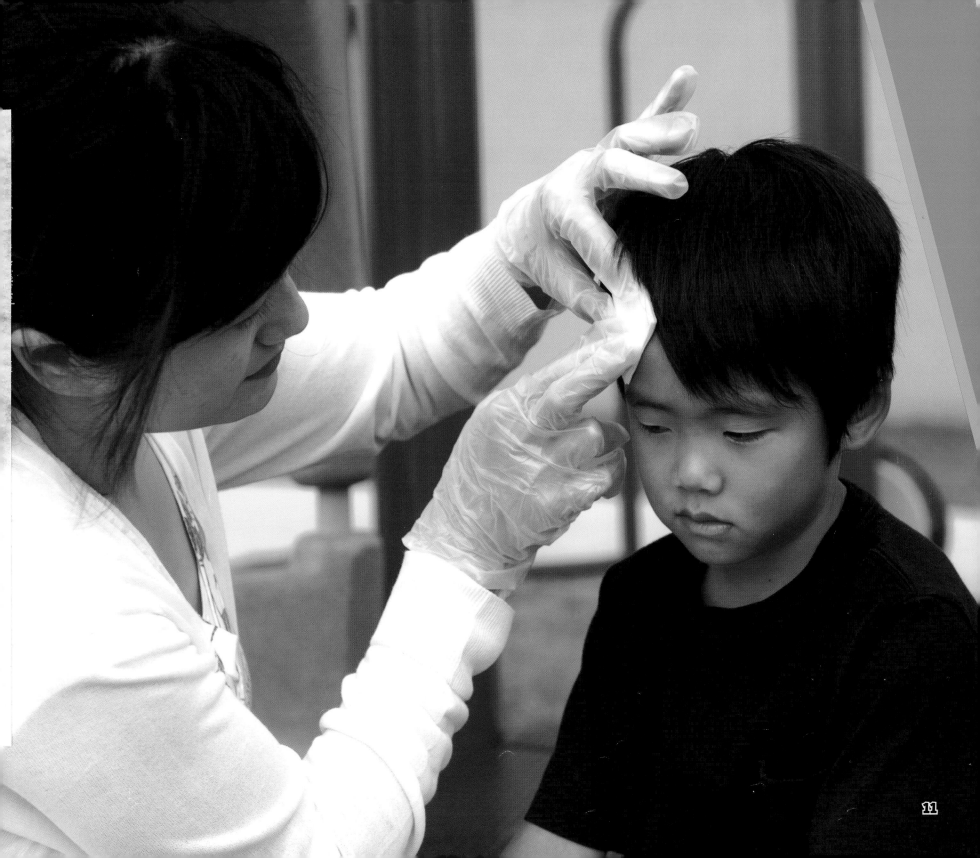

Nosebleeds

A person with a nosebleed
should sit down and
lean forward. The person then
pinches the soft part of the nose
until bleeding stops.

Bee Stings

Most bee stings just hurt. But some people swell up a lot. They may itch or have trouble breathing. They could have an allergy. Call 911 right away.

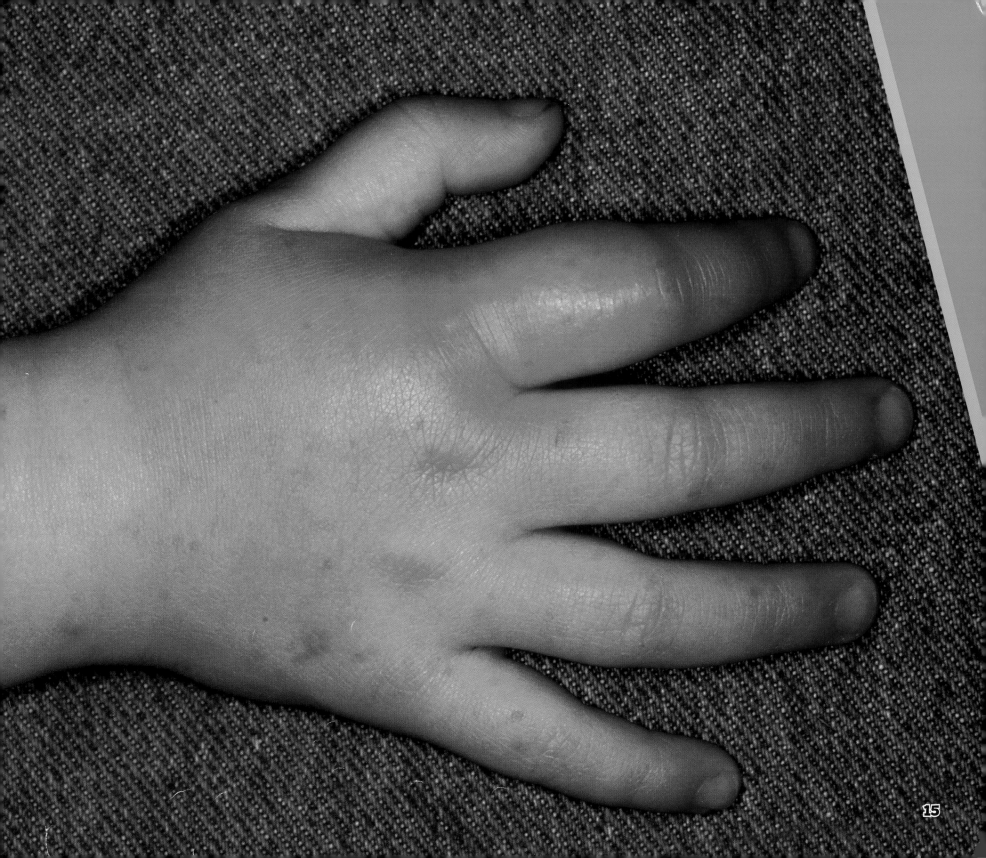

15

Bites

Always wash a bite and stop the bleeding. Bites from strange dogs or cats, ticks, and wild animals can be dangerous. The person should see a doctor.

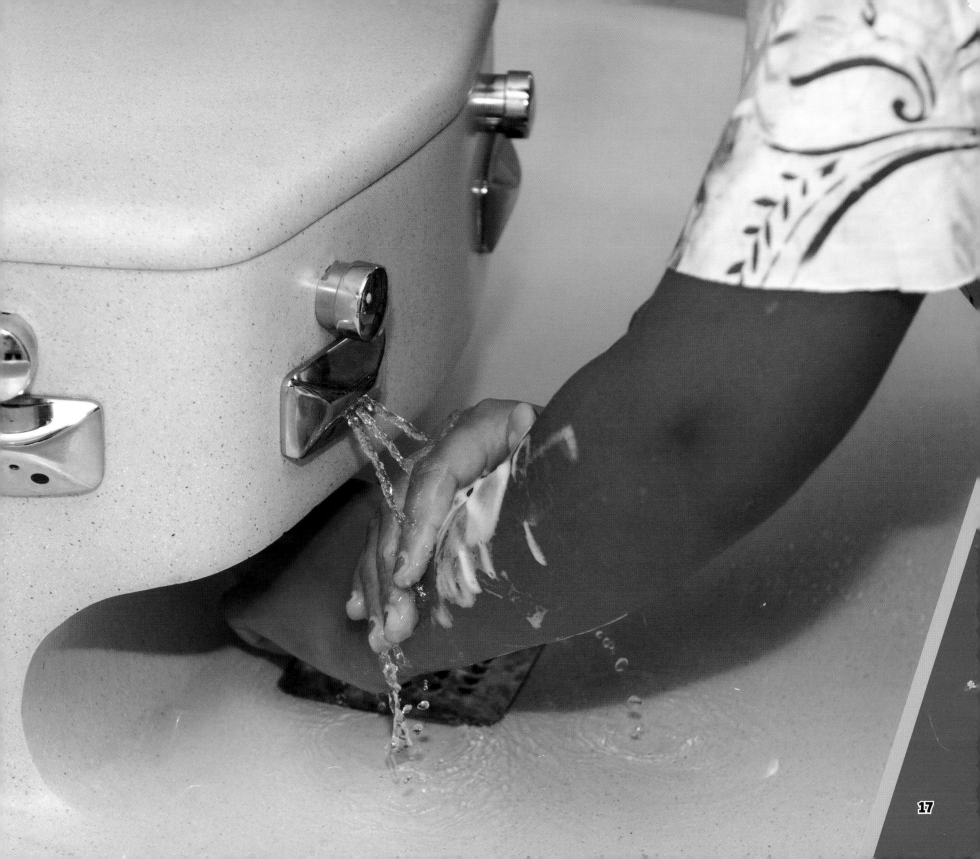

Choking

Someone who can cough or make sounds while choking can breathe. The person should stay calm and cough to clear the item.

A choking person who can't breathe may need the Heimlich maneuver from an adult. This action helps remove the choking object from the throat.

Glossary

allergy—having a reaction to something that is harmless to most people; people may be allergic to plants, animals, dust, or foods

bandage—a piece of material that covers cuts and other wounds

barrier—something that prevents other things from going past it; people giving first aid use gloves, bandages, or another barrier between their hands and blood

Heimlich maneuver—an emergency action done to remove an object from the windpipe; it is performed by squeezing the person from behind, below the ribs, with a quick motion

sting—to hurt with a poisoned tip

tick—a very small insect that looks like a spider; ticks suck blood from animals and people

Read More

Gorman, Jacqueline Laks. *Doctors.* People in My Community. New York: Gareth Stevens Pub., 2011.

Guard, Anara. *What If You Need to Call 911?* Danger Zone. Mankato, Minn.: Picture Window Books, 2012.

Nelson, Robin. *Staying Safe in Emergencies.* Health. Minneapolis: Lerner Publications Co., 2006.

Internet Sites

FactHound offers a safe, fun way to find Internet sites related to this book. All of the sites on FactHound have been researched by our staff.

Here's all you do:

Visit *www.facthound.com*

Type in this code: 9781429676953

Super-cool stuff! Check out projects, games and lots more at www.capstonekids.com

23

Index

Word Count: 232

Grade: 1

Early-Intervention Level: 20